ESCAPE

BLACK MOUNTAIN

CONTENTS

Written and illustrated by

Martin Chatterton

CHAPTER ONE

Mr Zim looked like someone had started out to make a grizzly bear before changing their mind and coming up with a teacher instead. He was big and kind of baggy and really, *really* forgetful.

However, there was one thing that Mr Zim never forgot and that was the camping trip.

Every spring, Mr Zim took Class 3F camping on Black Mountain next to Trout River. Up by the old red barn they would camp and fish and canoe, tell scary stories and toast marshmallows, and generally mess about like nobody's business.

Last year's camp was the best time 3F had *ever* had and they all agreed that Mr Zim was the greatest teacher in the history of the universe. Except, perhaps, for your teacher.

Even though Mr Zim was the greatest teacher in the history of the universe he wasn't perfect. For instance, he'd almost turned this year's trip into a total disaster when he forgot that he was getting married to Miss Floom *the exact same week as the camp.* It's hard to believe that anyone could forget something as important as getting married but Mr Zim did. That's just how he was.

When Miss Floom found out about Mr Zim's mistake she had gone absolutely bananas but, in the nick of time, Mr Zim had switched things around.

Now he and Miss Floom were getting married the day *after* camp finished. Miss Floom was almost as happy about it as Class 3F.

Almost. Camp was still camp, after all.

Class 3F were already having a totally terrific time at camp when something extra special happened.

At exactly two-thirteen on Wednesday afternoon, while everyone was playing in the field next to the red barn, a fat white snowflake landed on Chelsea Squarepoint's nose. It was only a snowflake but, because Chelsea Squarepoint was an A-grade attention-seeker, she screamed like a wounded buffalo.

"It's *freezing!*"
"No kidding," muttered Harry Wilson.

Harry scooted his chair past Chelsea Squarepoint
and Kellie Metropolis and their crowd of squealy
friends and picked up the Frisbee. He threw it
back to his best friend, Sally Pepper (who everyone
called 'Salty'), and looked up at the sky.

Another snowflake fell and then a couple more.

It was hard to believe but it was actually snowing!
It had never snowed at camp before!

"Is it going to snow, Mr Zim?" said Harry.
"Properly, I mean? Like deep, sticky, real
snowball-type snow?"

Mr Zim picked a cookie crumb out of his beard and absent-mindedly popped it in his mouth.

"Hmm," he said and looked up at the sky. "Snowball-type snow, eh?"

Harry waited patiently. You couldn't hurry Mr Zim when he was thinking.

"I'm edging towards a negative, Harry," said Mr Zim eventually. "It's far too warm. If it snows properly tonight I'll eat my undies."

CHAPTER TWO

Mr Zim opened his eyes and blinked.

For some reason, the roof of his tent was brushing the tip of his nose. When he'd gone to sleep the tent had been a normal distance from his nose.

"Extraordinary," said Mr Zim.
"Most peculiar."

He slid out of his sleeping bag
and crawled towards the tent opening.
Mr Zim slid the zip up and found
himself looking at a solid wall
of white stuff.

Snow. Lots and lots and lots of snow.

Mr Zim sighed. He wondered what his undies would taste like.

Outside, Class 3F were so happy they could hardly speak.

SNOW! *Snowsnowsnowsnowsnowsnow!*

It had come down in the night: a deep, sticky, proper snowbally snowfall. It lay in fluffy white drifts against the barn and thick slabs of it overhung the barn roof. The trees in the woods looked like they'd been dusted with icing sugar.

Aldo McPherson had to be dug out of his sleeping bag when his tent had ripped under the weight of snow. *That's* how much snow there was.

Now Class 3F were throwing snowballs and building snowmen and diving into snowdrifts and making snow angels like their lives depended on it. Snow was the best! Snow was awesome! This was the best camp of all time!

"We have to go home," said Mr Zim. "Right away."

Class 3F all stopped throwing snowballs and building snowmen and diving into snowdrifts and making snow angels.

Had they heard right? Had Mr Zim *really* suggested they stop having all this FUN and head back home?

"We have to get back before the old bridge gets blocked," said Mr Zim. "Sorry, 3F. Let's pack up."

Class 3F all glared at Mr Zim.

Mr Zim was the *worst* teacher in the history of the universe.

Mr Zim got everyone and their things loaded onto the bus in double-quick time.

"*Please* let us stay, Mr Zim!" wailed Class 3F. "*Puh—leeeeeeeease!*"

"No, 3F," said Mr Zim, in his super-serious voice. "We can't risk getting stuck up here." Class 3F didn't like what they heard but they kept quiet.

There was just enough bear in Mr Zim for
no-one to argue with him when he used his
super-serious voice.

Mr Zim started the engine and Class 3F
headed down the mountain in a silence far, far
frostier than the snow outside.

CHAPTER THREE

The rickety old bridge was covered in snow
and ice. It looked like it would collapse if so much
as another snowflake landed on it.

"That doesn't look safe, Mr Zim," said Harry.
"Maybe we should stay at camp?"

Mr Zim opened his mouth to say something
and then closed it again. A picture flashed into
his mind of Class 3F falling into Trout River
as the bridge collapsed.

Then he saw another picture of Miss Floom dressed in a wedding gown and looking at her watch. Her face was very red.

"Nonsense!" he said. "This bridge has been here for years. They don't make them like this any more. We're going across!"

Mr Zim drove slowly onto the bridge. Beneath the wheels of the bus the snow squeaked and the old planks groaned.

"Uh-oh," said Harry. He looked at Aldo and raised his eyebrows.

"Don't panic," said Mr Zim. "This bridge is as safe as –"

Just then, there was an almighty **CRACK** and the bus lurched suddenly to one side.

Everyone screamed.

Through the window Harry watched a couple of snow-covered planks tumble down, down, down into the river far, far below.

"Everybody off!" yelled Mr Zim.

It took about two seconds for Class 3F to get off the bus and back to the safety of the road.

"Everyone okay?" said Mr Zim.

He waved his phone in the air like a sword.

"I have a great plan," he announced. "I'll — yaroo!"

Class 3F never found out what Mr Zim's great plan was because, as he was speaking, he slipped on the snow and his legs shot straight up in the air. Mr Zim's phone flew out of his hand and into the river, and his head hit the back of the bus with a loud *clang*.

There was a short silence and then the bus started rolling slowly across the bridge: Mr Zim had forgotten to put the brake on.

When the bus reached the middle, the old bridge began to fall apart with a horrible creaking sound. "What do we *do*, Mr Zim?" shouted Class 3F. Mr Zim didn't reply because he had been knocked out cold when he banged his head.

Class 3F watched the bus containing all their clothes, food and phones hit the icy water and disappear forever.

They were trapped.

CHAPTER FOUR

Class 3F dragged Mr Zim back to the red barn and held an emergency meeting.

"Okay," said Harry, "anyone got any ideas?"

Everyone started speaking at once. As far as Harry could make out, most people wanted to wait in the barn until help arrived. Once Class 3F and Mr Zim didn't show up on Friday their parents would send out a rescue party.

With the bridge gone it would take a while for the rescue party to reach camp but they'd all be safely back home by Saturday. Or Sunday. Monday at the latest.

It was a good idea.

Except for one teeny, tiny problem.

"Mr Zim will miss his wedding," said Salty. "And Miss Floom will be really sad."

Everyone looked at Mr Zim lying peacefully in a corner. "Floomy zoomy!" he said, smiling. "Bananas on rollerskates." Although it was good that Mr Zim was awake, he was not making much sense.

"We *have* to get him back," said Harry.

"Why don't we see what's left in the barn?" said Aldo. "There's bound to be something we can use."

This is what was in the barn:

 A wonky torch

Fifteen old tennis rackets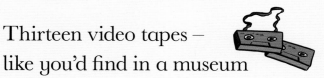

Thirteen video tapes –
like you'd find in a museum

A packet of stale biscuits

 A DVD without a box

A tube of super glue

An old painting table

A box of smelly old trainers

Four large metal trays

A map of Black Mountain
printed in 1972

Eight cardboard
boxes of newspapers

A stinky old duvet

 A thick knot of old TV cables

A heap of small stones

A dead mouse

Class 3F looked at the pile of stuff.

"We'll never get down the mountain with this heap of rubbish!" said Chelsea Squarepoint. "I vote we stick with Plan A and stay right here!"

"Chelsea's right," said Aldo. "This stuff's no good for anything."

It hurt Harry to admit it, but Chelsea had a point.

They had to stay. Plan A it was.

That night was the worst night in the history of the universe.

For a start, all 3F had to eat was half a stale biscuit each. If they needed a drink they had to suck handfuls of snow which only made them more thirsty. Then the lousy torch had gone out after about an hour leaving them in total darkness. Everyone was hungry and cold and thirsty and more than a little bit scared.

Worst of all, to keep warm, they had all had to *snuggle*.

Under the stinky duvet.

It was *way* beyond gross. It was triple gross.

By the time morning came *no-one* in Class 3F thought staying at the barn until Saturday was a good idea.

It was time to come up with a Plan B.

Which is exactly what they did.

CHAPTER FIVE

Nothing was wasted. Plan B needed everything they'd found in the barn.

First they all stuffed newspapers inside their clothes to keep warm.

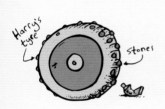

Then they superglued small stones to the fat tyres on Harry's chair to help it grip the snow better.

Mr Zim, wrapped in the stinky duvet, was fastened to a sled made from the old paint table using TV cables. The sled itself was attached to Harry's chair using some more TV cables. Salty tied some old trainers to the sled with bits of videotape to protect it from rocks and trees.

Aldo, Salty, Chelsea and Kellie used the old trays as snowboards, and everyone else fastened the tennis rackets to their feet to act as snow shoes. They were ready.

"Ready?" shouted Harry.

"READY!" roared Class 3F.

"I'm the king of Spain!" yelled Mr Zim.
"Take me to the palace!"

Mr Zim still wasn't quite himself. So far this
morning he'd been a gorilla, a Russian cosmonaut,
someone called Auntie Susan and now it seemed he
was the king of Spain.

"And are *you* ready, Your Majesty?"
said Harry.

"The king of Spain is *always* ready!"
yelled Mr Zim. "Vamos!"

Harry checked the old map one last time.
An old track led down and around the mountain.
It was steep in spots but going this way meant
they didn't have to cross the river. Harry pressed
a button on his chair and, with snow falling
heavily, 3F headed out of camp.

Plan B worked like a dream.

When the track was
blocked by a fallen tree
Class 3F had the answer.

When a hungry
wolf who had escaped from
a nearby safari park popped up from behind
a tree, the dead mouse came in very handy.

At the bottom of Black
Mountain it had stopped
snowing, so they used the
DVD to reflect the sun and
attract the attention of
a passing farmer.

The farmer loaded Class 3F into his truck and gave them a lift into town where everybody was very surprised and happy to see them, especially Miss Floom.

It was the best mountain escape plan in the history of the universe.

And the very next day, Miss Floom became the queen of Spain.